I Will Win

My Battle against Multiple Sclerosis

Saurabh Chowdhry

Dedication

I wholeheartedly dedicate this book to my parents, Rajesh and Madhu Chowdhry, for their unparalleled help and support with helping me live with MS.

I also dedicate this book to my brother and sister in law, Rahul and Samy Chowdhry, who are always there to help me if needed.

Last but not least, I also dedicate this book to anyone who suffers from MS or any disease. Health is wealth, so please take care of yourself.

Acknowledgments

I'd like to acknowledge my family and friends for their continued support in my battle against this disease and preventing it from taking control of my life.

About the Author

I began writing this book after years of disappointment, be it health-related or simply trying to get back all that I have lost.

It has become an all-encompassing whirlwind of events, and I'm trying my best to find solace in the things I can do.

I've painfully learned that life is not simple; rather, it is a struggle. But at the same time, I'm grateful for all that I have and all I can do.

This book is a reflection of my 'never give up' attitude coupled with my everlasting chase to be the best that I can be. To a clinician, MS stands for Multiple Sclerosis, but to me, it is a Minor Setback.

Having MS has instilled in me a newfound never give up attitude that reinforces my mental and physical attitude. I have come to accept that I am unable to do things as easily as I could before and have found gratitude in all that I'm still able to do. I have always aimed for perfection and I will not back down.

Preface

I have put my heart and soul into this book while recounting the highs and lows of my life, especially after I found myself battling with Multiple Sclerosis (MS), which I got diagnosed with nearly 20 years ago.

Since then, I believe it has been a roller-coaster ride. There have been so many challenges, setbacks, and inner turmoil, but I did not let them bring me down. I have triumphed over these challenges and emerged stronger.

I am not afraid of my illness; I have nothing to hide. I know perfection does not exist, so I have tried to do the next best. If I have won, great! If I haven't, this too is a lesson for me. I just take satisfaction in knowing that I did everything I could.

Contents

Page Left Blank Intentionally

Chapter 1
My Life, My Story

"Life is complicated. It starts before we're ready, it continues while we're still trying to figure out the point of it. And it ends long before we've worked out just what to do."

-Adrian Tan

Life is not easy; that is the fact that most of us can agree on. But what makes this life so difficult? Have you ever wondered why it is so complicated? It seems this is the only question that no one in the entire universe can answer. I wonder if it is our desire to reach the top and be the best version of ourselves. Us human beings are obsessed with the idea of success. We think our entire world will come crashing down if we do not find success. So we seek it everywhere, in our relationships, at work, and even at home. We push ourselves beyond our boundaries. Maybe that is why we find life so hard.

We do not take things easy. That leaves us exhausted in the process. However, that may not be the case for everyone. Maybe, what makes life hard is also our acceptance. We wonder if where we are is where we will be forever. We accept this fact, and so we do not strive to do better. We accept mediocrity, and in some cases, we even celebrate it. This makes life hard because who can always be happy with mediocrity when we are conditioned since birth to think otherwise? These are the questions that need to be answered, but who will answer them? Each one of us is living our life. We all are busy with it, and in some cases, completely lost in it. I am not trying to lay the blame on anyone. It is a fact. We all have our needs. When we are faced with a challenge, what do we do? Do we panic and retreat? Do we face it? Because, to us, running away is not the solution. Do we ignore the whole ordeal because, for us, denial works best? Again, where do we turn to find the answer? Is there an answer? Not all things in this world have one. Sometimes, we just accept what is not in our control and try to move on. If there is even an answer, is this good for everyone? The world does not follow a one-size-fits-all approach. Different things work for different people.

There is also another way to look at it. Maybe the answer is with us; we know it deep down. We just need to know how to access it. This leads me to my next question…what must we do to unravel the answer? There is no map that can provide us with the way. If we want the answer, we need to figure out how to get it ourselves. Some of us have dealt with a medical challenge with no known cure. Does this make the challenge tougher? Does it make it unique? Some people certainly think so. Then there are the luckier ones. They are lucky because they have easier challenges. I am talking about medical challenges. Sometimes, these are so easy that these can be fought head-on by taking a particular pill to soothe the pain or discomfort. This is how easy it is. A simple pill to swallow and the illness goes away—no side effects, nothing. Still, for some, it is not so simple. They have an illness so severe that there is no cure in sight. So they make peace with it and live life to the fullest.

Then there are conditions where a pill per se does not help. So, what can be done to provide help here? Doctors prescribe medicine to help mitigate the pain. The patient recovers after a while, or maybe the pill overpowers the senses of the patient until they no longer feel anything. In some cases, the pain is chronic but not so life-threatening, so the person continues to live with it in misery. Perhaps, the person resigns themselves to the idea of pain and somehow makes peace with it. But only a few brave men can do so. For the vast majority, it is not so easy. There is another scary scenario, which terrifies a lot of people. That is, what if there is no medicine to help? What if the illness you have is so rare that science has not started working on it at all? Only a few 100 people in the world ever have it, so science has decided not to spend too many resources on it. Another scenario comes to mind. What if the intended medicine does not offer any help? What if we keep on consuming the medicine in the hopes that we will get better, but we never do? Instead, we are stuck in a vicious cycle, wondering if we will ever get better.

What if the medicine that is supposed to help has its own course of side effects, which are more unbearable than the actual disease itself? It is said that the side effects of chemotherapy are horrible. People say it destroys life. It is far worse than cancer. Constant nausea, vomiting, weakness, and who can forget dizziness? People still choose to live with cancer and succumb to it. Oncologists themselves, when diagnosed with this deadly disease, choose to overlook chemotherapy altogether. Sure, they tell their patients that it is the best way forward, but do all of them live by this principle when they are diagnosed with a deadly illness?

These are a few questions some of us may have. I seek answers to these questions. I have a lot of what-ifs in my mind. It seems as if the scenarios keep piling up in my head. Maybe some of you can relate, maybe most of you can't.

College

In college, I decided to major in Biochemistry. So, I worked as a student researcher in a lab at the Department of Pathology of the medical school during my sophomore through senior years. This experience was amazing. The head (principal investigator) of the laboratory was great, as were the medical students coming into the lab. They were all incredibly helpful. I never felt out of place there. I had a sense of belonging. It was a second home for me.

The college campus was huge in every sense of the word. Tall buildings, long pathways, and even taller trees. It was open and spacious. It allowed me to move freely. I walked a lot. It was cathartic. The medical school campus where I worked as a student researcher was a good walk away, but I could walk the distance. I found the walk to open up my mind. I would go to the lab to do my research approximately three to four days a week.

Most of the time, I would grab dinner at the hospital cafeteria and stay at the lab studying past midnight. I had realized early on that the environment was peaceful. It allowed me to retain my course material. The same could not be said if I tried to study in the library or my room. Over here, I also had the luxury to use whatever equipment I could to help me learn. I would write notes on my boss' wash-erase board in his office, making sure not to accidentally erase any of my boss' notes. That would have caused a lot of problems for me. So I was extremely careful never to do that. I also made it a habit to leave his office neat and tidy. I felt a sense of duty. If he allowed me the flexibility to use his office at my will, I needed to show that I would not take advantage of it.

I can say that working in this lab made my college years undoubtedly great. While other students were busy partying and making their college years all about having fun, I was learning and having fun with my colleagues. The environment in this lab with my boss and medical students was great. We all got along extremely well. We were always joking around.

Being in that environment and around such people helped me grow. It has shaped me to be the person I am today. That much I can say. I took classes at the college alongside working at the laboratory. I guess this was where I spent most of my time in college, as it was where I studied all night. Yes, I rarely went to the library at the college campus but chose to study here. As I mentioned earlier, I absorbed more here. I guess it's true what they say, the place where one sits does have an impact on their psyche. I stayed in the lab, studying from about 7 P.M. until 1-2 A.M. the next day. I had no idea where the time flew. There was no one in the pathology department at the time. When I used to leave, it was very scary. My imagination used to run wild with the possibilities of what lurked in the silent corridors. I can still remember my footsteps echoing in the silence. I often wondered what would happen if I heard a second pair of footsteps echoing behind me, knowing that no one but me came to this place at this time of night. It is a good thing that I never had to experience that.

As soon as I exited the lab, I would take the elevator to go down from the ninth floor. When I would come out of the elevator, it was pitch dark, as there was never any sound of any type. Here my imagination used to run wild again. Although it was funny, this never stopped me from going back or even leaving the lab early. I used to walk back very quickly to the college campus. It is somewhat odd when I look in retrospect as I was never scared walking back to my dorm that late. It felt natural to roam the silent campus. I wonder why I did not feel the same way when I exited the lab. However, stress never took the front seat during my college years as I was so relaxed throughout. You hear other people sweating it, studying all the time, and still not making it through. These people are stressed all the time, but this was never me. I was extremely relaxed throughout.

One day, it all changed. There was a particular time when I was doing my research. While holding a pipette in my hand and doing an experiment, my hand began to tremor. I was very confused about this sensation, but since this was the first time this happened to me, I did not read too much into it. However, I did make it a point to go and meet my doctor. So when I went home the following weekend, I went to see my doctor and ask him for his opinion. He mentioned the shaking in my hand could possibly be a sign of multiple sclerosis (MS). I was a bit shocked and fearful but did not think too much about it.

After going back to school the following week, I shared what my doctor said about MS with my lab boss and medical students who worked in the lab. They all laughed and denied the possibility of my symptoms being related to MS. It was almost like a joke to them. Everyone was dismissive. No one entertained the idea that it could possibly be real or that it could have such a big impact on my life. It was unbelievable, to say the least.

Medical School

Many people in my extended family, as well as my friends' circle, are physicians. I also have a love for science. So my decision to pursue a career in medicine came naturally. There was no confusion or doubt. I knew what I had to do and did not waste time dwelling on the different paths I could tread. So, upon graduating from college, I applied to medical school to fulfill my dream of becoming a physician.

Although the decision to attend medical school was easy for me, the process was extremely demanding. It was exhausting both mentally and physically. The process demanded that the applicant had to be not only an excellent student but also an all-rounder. This means he/she had to be involved in student societies, extracurricular activities, while maintaining a near-perfect GPA, etc. Only a few ones can manage this while carrying on with their social life.

Hence, I earnestly applied to different schools and fortunately was accepted to one of them. Medical school was absolutely great. Taking gross anatomy and being immersed in the smell of formaldehyde was enjoyable for me. I saw a cadaver for the first time in my life— the smell of formaldehyde sticks to your hair, skin (despite wearing gloves), etc. I still enjoyed it anyway. I felt I was learning.

Upon walking around the lab, looking at different cadavers, I was in awe of how each and every human body has the same organ systems, whether it is respiration, digestion, etc. Take a moment to think about this. There are billions of people populating this planet. All have different external features, more or less. However, if you cut open the inside, you will find we all are the same, down to the last artery.

It was only after seeing a cadaver that I was in awe of the complexity and purposefulness of different systems of this perfect machine called the human body. When given the scalpel to begin dissecting, I was completely amazed. Cutting the rib cage and exposing the heart and lungs is a sight so powerful that it cannot be expressed in words. One has to experience this to know what I mean. This is the set of organs that keeps us alive every second and every minute of every day. They are always working, from the moment we are born until we die. They never rest, for if they do, we will end up dying.

It is amazing how the heart and lungs work together to deliver freshly inhaled oxygen throughout the body and get rid of the wasteful carbon dioxide. This perfect machine is surely a divine creation that no human can replicate ever.

Chapter 2
Slowly but Surely

*"Never be afraid to fall apart because it is an opportunity
to rebuild yourself the way you wish had been all along."*

-Rae Smith

Little did I know that my struggle was only beginning.
The symptoms I had felt earlier were going to transform into
a life-changing illness for me. However, I managed to
navigate through it, though at the time, it felt impossible. My
problems started to increase as time went on. I had just come
from visiting the doctor when I was on vacation and resumed
school. I vividly recall that was the ending of the first
semester, and for some reason, I was beginning to feel
sluggish.

This was particularly worse when I was walking. At the
same time, I was starting to have a double vision, pins and
needles sensation, and balance/coordination issues. I was
wondering what exactly was going on with me. I thought
back to things that could have led me to this position. But I
could not pinpoint exactly what I had done wrong.

My personal life also started to suffer. Of course, it was bound to happen. It was not as if the symptoms knew how to distinguish between my personal and sick lives. It was getting so bad that the girl I was dating at the time started to stay away from me. This made me feel more hopeless and depressed. I remembered the quote I had once read. That kept me going.

"No storm, not even the one in your life, can last forever. The storm is just passing over."

-Iyanla Vanzant

I took refuge in this quote. There was something about it that provided me with a lot of hope and comfort. At the same time, my desperation knew no bounds. I needed to know what the problem was with me. Why could I not get a proper diagnosis? I started to camp out in the medical library and went through several medical books. I needed to find other patients like myself. I wanted to ask them badly about the symptoms that they were going through, the emotions that were running through their minds and, more importantly, how they were dealing with it. I even turned to my professors to discuss my symptoms. I wanted their opinion on the symptoms I was having.

One of my professors suggested it was Bells Pasley, but he was unsure. He needed scans to make a proper diagnosis. I continued to do my research, hoping I would find a cure, one that would eliminate my symptoms with a single pill. However, it was not going to be that easy. I could feel that in my bones.

My knees were growing weak as I sat on the library floor with the journal that was giving me a detailed view of my symptoms along with the possible diagnosis. As I read through the possibilities, there was an inner turmoil rising within me. I felt dread, despair, anger, and hurt. I felt a strong sense of resentment, even toward God. I was not a bad person. I was not a killer. I did not hurt people. I was not the deceiver.

It seemed I was paying off the sins of another person. Why me? I was a good person. I was to dedicate my life to helping other people. I was striving to become a doctor who could save lives. But who would save mine? It seemed as if the tables had turned on me.

It was this realization that sent chills up and down my spine. I felt helpless. Whatever power I had been feeling, it had all disappeared — snatched away by the disease. At that point, I felt as if I had no options for myself because, to me, a doctor could never be a patient. I saw my dream crumble before my very eyes. It was like a glass I had in my hand that shattered into a million pieces. The pieces all covered the floor, some of them so tiny that they could never be put together again. This was how I felt about my life at the time. The pain in my chest was so severe that I could not even breathe. I needed to step away from this, and so, I went to a corner and cried my heart out. The medical journal slipped through my hands, so did my hopes, dreams, and aspirations. All was lost.

Added to this was the fact that I had an extended family that was counting on me. They wanted to support my dream of becoming a doctor. I thought of my parents, my brother, my girlfriends, and friends. We were all in this together. How would they react to having this dream crushed? How would I tell them? Who would deal with their reactions? I felt the world spin around me. I felt I needed to sit, or I would faint. I sat on the floor, my face buried in my hands. My thoughts then wandered to my girlfriend. What would she think? How would she react? Was she going to leave me or stick around for the long haul? At that time, I did not have a proper diagnosis. I knew my prognosis and had already decided what life was going to look like. To me, that was a death sentence. Looking back, I think I was too hasty to pass judgment. Things do get better, and the sun always does come out. We just have to be patient.

I got up and decided that if I could not have the life that culminated in my dreams, perhaps it was best that I stepped away from it altogether. This was not the life I wanted. I wiped my tears that were streaming down my face and walked to the dorm room. I was terrified. It seemed the terror was not going to subside, no matter what happened. I briefly contemplated suicide by running off the ledge. I was fed up of feeling this way.

I wanted the pain and suffering to end. To me, death was the only way out of this mess I was in. I mustered the strength and tried, but it did not work. A few students caught me just as I was going to jump. They wanted to know why I was doing this. They wanted to know what was so bad about my life that I had felt the need to end my life. I was feeling overwhelmed at that point. There was the stress of school, walking difficulties, not feeling well, and the confusion of what was happening around me. It all accumulated into making me feel lost, confused, and scared. There are no words that I can pen down to describe the emotional turmoil I was going through. It was as if there was a wall, and I could not see beyond that. The wall towered just a few inches over my face and seemed to go up forever. The heightened stress level was normal for me.

I could not function anymore and had still been a full-time student. So, I decided to withdraw. That was another painful decision for me. I did so without knowing what lay ahead of me. This, of course, led to increasing stress levels until it all snowballed, leading to a mental breakdown.

Chapter 3
The Road Ahead

"Maybe life is not about avoiding the bruises. Maybe it's about collecting the scars to prove that we showed up for it."

-Hannah Brencher

I returned home. I was slowly starting to process what was happening to me, though there were still times when I felt my brain had stopped working. There were moments when I felt that this was all just a dream, and a time would come when I would wake up only to realize that all this was just a dream. But nothing of the sort ever happened.

I met with my primary care physician. After discussing exactly what I was feeling, he decided to refer me to a neurologist. This neurologist scheduled me for a set of MRIs of my brain and spinal cord. When I went in for the MRI, I was fearful, although I knew on some level what was wrong with me. However, fear was almost second nature to me at this point. My brain and cervical spine's MRI scans showed several lesions, evidence of a demyelinating disease, namely multiple sclerosis. I have stated this repeatedly that I knew on some level what was going on inside my body. I was prepared for the diagnosis…or so I thought. But when the final verdict was given to me, I was emotionally distraught. I knew it was coming, but the information still hit me like tons of bricks. It seems as if we can prepare for the worst of all we want, but we can never predict what will happen once the worst stands in front of us. I had a neurological condition. There was a silver lining to it, I believe. I was finally aware of what my body was going through and what I was going through. The next step could then be taken, which was how to deal with it.

I had a very good friend. We used to play tennis on our school's tennis team. He saw how depressed I was and introduced me to the world of online dating. I had nothing to lose, so I pursued the girls. I began to talk with and later date a particular girl. This went on for a few years, during which she went to college and majored in accounting. She graduated pretty soon, and it was on her graduation day that she stopped by my house and introduced her parents. My parents met hers, and they talked about us getting married. I was very excited. It seemed as if I was finally catching a break from my illness and life in general. But I was getting ahead of myself. This was the point when her elder sister noticed a tremor in my head. She let it go, or maybe she went and told her parents because things soon started to unravel. The next night, her parents invited my family and me over for dinner. It was all going well, and soon it was time to leave. I grabbed my coat and headed out the door. It was then that the bombshell hit me, and my right leg started to tremble. It was dangerous. There were no railings, so I was in real danger of falling and hurting myself badly. What was happening? Fear and confusion started to set in.

My girlfriend's parents unexpectedly showed up at my house the very next day. They canceled all the plans for the wedding. I was devastated, and so was my girlfriend. However, we still continued our relationship despite the fact that her parents were against it. It got to the point that she decided that she would run away from her house for me. She felt she could no longer listen to her parents and be without me. I calmed her down and told her to face reality. I did the bravest thing and told her that she had to do as her parents said. I did not want a rift to be created between her and her parents because of me. I could not bear such responsibility.

Pretty soon, I got a job as a science editor for a major textbook company. My girlfriend got a job as an accountant. It was also around this time that I was going to graduate school to earn a master's degree in biology. I commuted from home via the local train. I was also very content with the fact that I could travel freely. I did not have to rely on other people to go to different places. However, I knew this sense of independence might not last for very long.

My job was awesome as it involved writing and editing chapters of a to-be-published science textbook. My duties also entailed selecting academic science manuscripts, which were lessons of chapters of a to-be-published science textbook. But things did not remain the same, as they never do. The science department of the company I was working for was taken over by another publishing company.

This resulted in a number of workers being laid off. I was one of them. This meant I had to search for a new job. Thus began the long and painful process of finding a job. At this time, however, my walking ability was not that bad, but I did have some balance issues. Overall, I was doing pretty well. Luckily, I got another job. I was hired by a very popular test prep company. I worked as an academic science editor for different scientific publications. I fell in love with this job. But again, I was laid off after a year of having worked there. I do not know why I was let go, but my gut tells me it was a result of my disability. I firmly believe that it is very difficult to have a job while being a disabled person. Once people see you walking a little bit differently or having a tremor, they do not want you to be a part of the company anymore. Sadly, that's the way the world works, I guess.

It had to be my disability because I know in my heart that I was not at fault. I came to work on time, and diligently worked all day. I also believe that certain employers do not want disabled people to work for them in any way. They look for reasons to let people like me go out of fear of a lawsuit. It was never my intention to sue anyone. In fact, the thought never even crossed my mind because I truly enjoyed the work that I did.

I believe it helped to prep future students. It was also because of this that I had decided to go into teaching. After I was let go and while I was still unemployed, I received an email about a graduate degree program in which I would be working as a student teacher during the day and taking classes in the night. I was happy beyond words. I could not believe that this opportunity had just dropped in my life. But there was a part of me that was scared. I did not know if I would be well received. I was walking with a cane at the time. I felt I would be laughed at by the students. So began the next chapter of my life working as a student-teacher. I enjoyed every second of it, even more so than my previous jobs. It was refreshing to teach and enlighten young minds.

Though I was tired, I enjoyed the whole thing. I taught each lesson with enthusiasm and treated each student as if they had something to offer to the class. There was mutual respect. I do not think I ever felt this comfortable and at ease during my entire life. The feeling I lived with was as if I was meant to do this. The whole experience felt like my life's purpose.

I went on to graduate and walked on the stage during the convocation, mostly because I was fully supported by my classmates, faculty, and other students. This time, I was not the least bit embarrassed about having a disability. I was very proud of the things I had accomplished. It is not easy to juggle a disability with a full-time job. I know now for sure that my unemployment was not my fault. Despite having two master's degrees, I did not have a proper job. Recruiters told me that I am regarded as a liability by the employees. It hurts me when I think about it, but I guess I have made my peace with life. Since it cannot be proven, I smiled and simply accepted it. I try not to let these things bring me down. Life is very tough. We cannot allow other people to control our worth. My walking has worsened in recent years despite the fact that I take medicine, exercise, and go for physical therapy religiously. But I will never give up. I have no intention of doing so. As in the words of Vince Lombardi, *"It's not whether you get knocked down; it's whether you get up."*

Chapter 4
Sports

"Winners never quit and quitters never win."

-Vince Lombardi

I have always loved to play sports. Whether it was baseball, football, or tennis, I enjoyed every second of it, although it did not come without its fair share of injuries. I mean, there were times when I broke my collarbone or wrist, but that never deterred me. I loved the thrill of running around and going up against my mates. That passion was always there.

Playing sports was a big deal, as was watching sports. It did not matter to me if my favorite team never won the World Series or the Super Bowl. I watched it for enjoyment purposes and rooted for my favorite team, waiting for their next big win. Now, I have MS. This means I cannot even dare to dream of playing any sport.

When I was playing for my high school tennis team, we won our division of the championship and played the finals at the US Open site in New York. It was truly a memorable moment. I am truly grateful that I got to experience that moment. I am also grateful for the fact that my MS symptoms did not start showing up until later. If they would have, perhaps this was something I would never have been able to experience or have a memory of. It was only years later that newfound symptoms showed up. I was playing tennis casually one time and seeing two balls instead of only one, and I would make a regular attempt to hit the ball but ended up missing and swinging in the air. This was while I was in med school.

The game was going on, and my opponent and I were hitting the ball back and forth like we usually do. I was completely into the game, never taking my eyes off the ball for even one second. Suddenly, something happened. Instead of one ball, I saw two balls hurling toward me. I blinked my eyes and shook my head, but there were still two balls coming toward me.

As a result, I missed swinging in midair. Little did I know that this was the beginning of a lifelong illness. It was one of the first MS symptoms I had before the diagnosis. But at the time, I did not think much of it. The double vision went within a couple of minutes, and I blamed it on the lack of sleep. As I write this, I look back and feel a whole new level of gratitude that I was able to enjoy my younger years without having to worry about when the next symptom would show, where it would show, and whether I would need the help of random strangers to recover from it. The worrying has taken up much of my new time and energy, and I am left to wonder what path my life will take.

"Those good old days seem like so long ago."

-Deborah Cox

I keep up with daily exercises to make sure that I am as fit as is physically possible, given my condition. I get on the treadmill every day so that I can walk properly. I also use the recumbent bike to keep my leg muscles from reaching atrophy. There are a few things under my control. I get to decide how active my body can be with MS, so I have made these things part of my daily routine.

I want to live a long and healthy life as much as I can. I understand that some of the activities are just too strenuous for my body to handle, but I know I can still enjoy the little things in life. The thing is, no one can be certain of what tomorrow will bring. Perhaps tomorrow there will be a cure for MS. There was a time when the common cold killed people as there was no cure until there was. So I remain hopeful, as should you too, that there will be a tomorrow that can give you what you really desire. I have complete faith that something great will definitely come about. The least I can do is to keep up the movements of my legs. I love what Bernard F. Asuncion said, *"Practice like you've never won, perform like you've never lost."*

This is so quintessential of my mindset as, despite my failures with MS, I always keep trying to move one step ahead of where I was before. I am determined to make progress, even if it as little as a step forward. I just want to be one step ahead from yesterday. I feel this is the only way I can possibly beat MS and not let it beat me.

If MS thinks it can overpower me easily, it should think again. There is no way I will let it hijack my life. It showed up announced, ready to stay. But I am more armored now. I am determined to win this battle. This time, it will be MS that has to find a way out because it is no longer welcome inside my body.

Chapter 5
Family & Medicines

"There is no failure except in no longer trying."

- Elbert Hubbard

My younger brother got married. The event took place in Canada, but I was unable to attend it. This was because I was in the hospital, suffering from a urinary tract infection. My parents have always been helpful and supportive of my illness, and so has my dog Pepsi. He is our family dog. I have spent a lot of time with him. I must say he truly is an awesome friend.

Pepsi was very attached to me. The more time I spent with him, the more our emotional bond grew stronger. I used to take him for his nightly walks before bedtime. He was so well aware of my situation that he did not even try to pull the leash. He would also feel my suffering I went through. He was a true friend. It hurts me to say that he passed away just a couple of months ago because of blood cancer. He is and will always be missed.

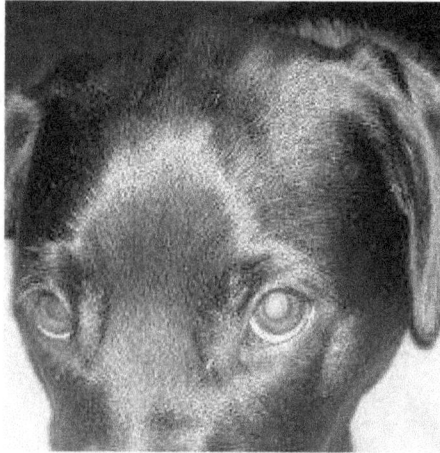

Pepsi used to run to greet us as soon as we came back home. He would greet us at the door and run around in circles to show us how happy he was. He was aware of the fact that my bed was the only bed that he could sleep on, so he would take his daily naps on my bed. I miss his warm presence. He was extremely smart and never slept on my pillow. Instead, he took the small space reserved for him on the foot of my bed. He even knew how to shake his hands. He would lift one of his paws and place it in my hands lovingly. I consider him an integral part of my family; we all do. I am very close with my siblings and have nothing but love for them in my heart. My younger brother, who was getting married at the time, is great. He has always been there to help me out.

My sister-in-law is also a terrific person who is always full of humor, joy, and compassion. She knows I can use humor in my life, so she never disappoints. With her, I never felt that she would say no to any of my demands. Not that I have many demands - I am fortunate enough to be able to do everything on my own – but the point is, she gives me this sense of security.

Not one of the medications for MS has managed to help me out because I am dealing with multiple things at one point. There is my gait I have to watch out for and also my balance and coordination. If these are not aligned, I can topple over anytime. In all honesty, it is not as if I have not given these medications a chance. I have tried all the allopathic MS medications that my doctor ever gave to me.

Upon my diagnosis, my neurologist even prescribed me an interferon called Avonex. I took it regularly for a year, but it gave me the flu-like side effects and made me feel miserable. I could not cope with that.

A few patients react very well to this drug, but I was not one of those. After I complained to my neurologist about the side effects of using this medicine, he decided to switch me to another medicine, Beta Seron. This was not much of an improvement. It was an interferon once again, but a different one. This one also had horrible side effects, but at least it was not as bad as the first one. I felt I could still tolerate this, to an extent.

Regardless, the side effects were still there, so I was unable to continue for much longer. Then, my neurologist put me on synthetic MS medicine, which was to be self-injected under the skin every single day. It was annoying, not to mention painful, but I did this for a little over a year. The good thing was that the side effects were not as bad, but my health still deteriorated.

So this one time, I was stuck in the hospital and watching Dr. Oz on television. Coincidentally, he had two guests, both of who had MS. The only difference was that one of the guests was taking an allopathic MS medication, and the other was taking homeopathic medicine. The surprising thing was that both guests seemed to be happy about their choice of medicine. I decided to look into it, as I was getting quite exhausted by using western medicine. I googled MS and homeopathy on my phone and sent the information I stumbled upon to my brother. There was a well-known homeopathic doctor in Montreal who specialized in treating MS. My family and I decided to drive all the way to Montreal so that we could meet with this doctor.

Soon, I started to take the homeopathic medicines and continued to do so for over a year. However, the results were not what I expected. Instead of the smooth road to recovery, my health started to get worse. I was not responding to the treatment at all. It did not matter if it was homeopathy or not. I felt as if my system was failing me, that MS had finally won, and I was weak. Still, I did not give in to despair. I continued with my plan of action. Even though I was exhausted and felt unable to do anything, I emailed my cousin at Harvard and asked for his advice on the next steps to take. I figured he would know something. At that point, I was ready to try just about anything to make myself feel just a bit better. My cousin was not an MS specialist, but he worked for someone well-known for being an MS specialist. My cousin decided to ask his boss about what he could do. He was also there for me, responding to my needs. I believe I owe him a lot too. His boss advised that I should start taking an allopathic intravenous medicine called Rituxin and another medicine called Biotin. So I did just that. I went to a nearby infusion center to get my Rituxin infusions. At the same time, I also started to take Biotin three times a day in addition to Vitamin D and B-12. My neurologist told me that the way Rituxin works helps prevent the human body from further damage caused by MS.

Despite everything I have taken, I strongly believe that I am unable to tell just how much medicine is working. However, I am hopeful. I believe that I will eventually find a drug that is suitable for me and will make me better. It just has to. I have far too much faith in God to think otherwise. Besides, to think differently is to walk down the path of depression, which I do not want to do. I do not want to succumb to depression. I believe I am allowed to scream and cry, but I do not have the luxury of giving up.

Chapter 6
My Dreams

"To uncover your true potential you must first find your own limits and then you have to have the courage to blow past them."

-Picabo Street

It is no surprise that I wanted to be a medical doctor. I have talked about this earlier also. My passion for becoming a doctor started since I was very young. I felt I could change the world, help people, and make a difference in their lives. Nothing would satisfy me more, I felt.

While in college, I worked as a researcher for three years in a lab in the Department of Pathology, which was run by an awesome principal investigator. Under his tutelage, my love for the medical sciences grew exponentially. I felt alive when I was working in that lab. You know, people find an escape from work. They do not want to give it more than the standard eight hours.

My case was different. I was willing to put in a lot more effort to understand this field. I felt as if my lab was my home away from the dorm room. I also had a key to the lab, so I could study there until past midnight. It was peaceful to be there. I felt as if I could think freely, perhaps even more freely than I was able to while I was in my dorm room.

Once I was done with the day, I would walk back to my room in the darkness of the night. There were only a few lights that would allow me to see my way. It was by working in this lab that my fascination for having a career as a physician-scientist was born. So, it was upon graduating from college that I did go to medical school. I was elated during this time. I felt as if my ambitions and dreams were finally coming together. In life, I finally had a purpose I could work toward. However, it was short-lived. Do you ever feel afraid of being too happy and fear that your happiness would soon end? I guess that was what I started to feel.

"I think I'm afraid of being happy because whenever I get too happy, something bad always happens."

-Charles M. Schulz

It was during this time, during my first year of medical school, that I began to feel weird. I started to have all of these odd symptoms. I was unable to walk properly. There were times I felt I would need a cane to walk just ten steps. I was not able to see properly, either. The double vision had become a frequent occurrence. I would be looking at my plate of food, and suddenly it would double. I had to blink a few times to clear my vision. There were also other cognitive difficulties. I knew something was off. I could feel it in my bones. I just did not know what it was. I often wondered what was happening to me. Would I get better, or was it something serious? The thoughts continued to plague me.

As time went on and the symptoms showed no signs of going away, I became increasingly concerned. I had no idea what to do or what steps to take. I could concentrate on nothing. Of course, this interfered in other parts of my life. My love life, for instance, took a toll. Matters with the girl I was dating at the time got worse unexpectedly. This stressed me out even more. I wondered if this illness would allow someone to fall in love with me and be by my side or not.

I still vividly remember the day when my blurry vision and lack of concentration became the cause of my accident. I slipped and banged my forehead on the marble-like kitchen floor and ended up getting several stitches. At that point, I wondered if things could get any worse. The worst part was,

I felt completely alone. There was no one to turn to, who could lift me or understand my pain. You could say I was lost, but '*I feel lost*' is an understatement. When one is lost, one can always find a way back. There are always people waiting for them. But I was feeling alone and lonely. I had no one I could tell what I was going through. I wouldn't lie, but that was when the thought of committing suicide crossed my mind several times. And only the thought convinced me to do so. I felt there was no point in living. This world had nothing to offer except pain and misery. I understood at that point why people killed themselves, why it was that they chose death instead of life. So, I decided to end my life. I can honestly tell you that once I decided that, I felt free. To know that I would not have to deal with these things felt oddly liberating. You know, I have heard that suicidal people feel elated when they decide to end their lives. It was like a huge burden of continuing to live was lifted off my shoulders.

So, I decided to jump, and I very nearly succeeded, except that a couple of students saw me. They came to me and notified the Dean. He took over the case and asked me to speak to him. He also ordered that I speak to the school psychiatrist. I had no option. My thoughts continued to plague me. Why was I feeling this way? Why was the entire universe against me? I had a nervous breakdown because I could not understand what I had done to deserve this.

This was a long time ago. Now I am grateful for the fact that I no longer have these thoughts. I am no longer suicidal. I feel grateful when I see people who are living with worse health conditions than I am. It is in these moments that I look up at the sky and feel grateful that God has blessed me with eyes to see the world around me. With ears to listen to different noises around me. With a mouth that allows me to breathe and speak freely. This makes me forget about MS. This makes me forget my sufferings. It is important to note that I was not stressed out because of my studies. The material came easy to me. I was stressed over these symptoms because I had no idea what they meant. So, after speaking with the Dean, I ultimately decided to withdraw from school, which I did.

Chapter 7
Relationships

"You can't control everything. Sometimes you just need to relax and have faith that things will work out. Let go a little and just let life happen."

-Kody Keplinger

When I was diagnosed, one of the areas of my life that had a definitive impact was my love life. Things were getting pretty serious with this girl, and we were planning on taking things to the next level. But there was something stopping us from getting to that level. It was mainly her parents. She knew that me telling them about MS would mean the end of our relationship.

At the time, we had been dating for seven years, and our families had already met. Still, my ex continued to stay silent on this matter. But the truth came out. It always does. It is only a question of when. I offered my ex's sister some treats while we were at one of our gatherings. Out of nowhere, my hands started to tremble. I cannot forget the look on her sister's face. She was shocked, to say the least. As for me, I decided not to show any concern for it. I laughed it off, hoping it would not prompt any more questions. Her parents then invited us over for dinner over the following weekend. Everything was going smoothly. Dinner was over soon, and we all got ready to go home. It was then that all hell broke loose. About four steps were going up to her front door without any handrails. When I started to walk down those stairs, anxiety, nervousness, and fear all got together, which led to my leg shaking uncontrollably. I managed to limp to our car, and we arrived back home. Her parents, however, did not miss this little incident. They came over the next day and canceled all the proposed plans that we had.

This crushed me entirely. We had been going through so much together, and it vanished into thin air. It was as if our relationship meant absolutely nothing. She was just as heartbroken as I was. She called me crying. I did not know what to do since I was in the same boat as her. At the time, I hated having this illness. I felt as if there was no bright side to it. Moreover, it cost me everything, including the person I had been in a relationship for the past seven years. So when my girlfriend was crying, I did not know how to react or what to say.

I knew her parents were strictly against this. I repeatedly asked myself where the love was. She claimed that her parents told her to choose me or choose them. There was no other option. When I heard this, I felt myself break even more. I succumbed to the loss. In retrospect, I looked back and wondered if she truly loved me at all. Love is about sticking with the person through the good and the bad. It is not about leaving them stranded because the parents said no. Did she actually believe that this was her way of letting me down? Did she ever love me at all, or had she just been playing me for the past seven years? I think I will never know the answer. I have to make peace with that fact.

As time went on, I moved on from this and went out into the dating field again. I started to date another girl who lived in Denver, Colorado. We hit it off. I went to Colorado to see her, and she came all the way to New York to hang out with me. We even scheduled a trip for Miami to have some fun. Along the way, I told her that she should inform her parents that I have MS to see if they would allow such a relationship to continue. I did not want to go through the same thing I went with my ex-girlfriend. It was painful and took me a long time to recover.

So she did inform her parents, and expectedly, they were not accommodating to the idea that their daughter would marry someone so sick. They did not want a sick person in the family. I often wondered if she actually told her parents about me, or did she back off on her own accord because she was scared. Maybe she did not see our relationship going too far.

There was another ex who was from medical school. We also hit it off. I could see this going somewhere. But I left school because the symptoms were getting the best of me. I could no longer maintain my balance properly, coordinate, or control my tremors. It was later that all of this led to the diagnosis of only one thing, which was MS. I can honestly say that the onset of MS and its symptoms made life difficult for me.

I could not keep myself grounded. I was constantly looking for relief, something that would make the symptoms manageable. I felt I had lost my grip on life. Along with this, my self-confidence took a hit, and I fell victim to feeling dazed, lost, and very confused. There were days when I did not even know who I was. Despite it all, I was never really upset. I was just lost and believed that I had not met the right girl yet, the girl who would walk by my side and not leave me because of MS That girl is out there waiting for me. I just know this. When the time is right, our paths will cross, and we will make it work. I have complete faith that all of this will happen at the right time and place. So it is useless for me to sit here and blame myself for all my relationships that failed because of MS. Who knows, maybe they would not have worked out even if I was not diagnosed with this life-altering disease. After all, no one really knows what life has in store for you.

Chapter 8
Fatigue

"Nature does not hurry, yet everything is accomplished."

-Lao Tzu

A number of things affect my daily living with MS-balance, coordination, and dexterity, to name a few. However, I firmly believe that fatigue tops the list. You see, I get tired very quickly, even when I am doing the smallest of things. You might think things like getting ready (showering, shaving, and putting on clothes) were part of my routine, so they would not take time. But it was not that way. There were times when it used to get too much for me to handle.

I used to come out of the bathroom, feeling so tired that I had to sit down on my bed for ten (10) minutes to catch my breath. Then and only then would I be able to function normally. Otherwise, I could not even dream of going through the rest of the day. There is another thing I suffer from as the MS symptoms continue to worsen. There is spasticity in my right leg. It comes to a point where I am unable even to lift my right toe. This happens only occasionally, but that is a reason enough to be concerned. It has become increasingly difficult for me to be able to step over the edge of the bathtub. It is like running a marathon. I am not exaggerating, but I sweat so much when I am trying to do a task as simple as lifting my right leg from the bathtub to the shower. It is easy when I have to do it with my other foot. I have no difficulties then. But with the other foot, it takes up my entire energy.

So I began to dread the mornings, knowing I would be out of energy before the day even started. This thought in itself was enough to make me not get out of bed. But then I realized that the stress was doing me absolutely no good at all. So I got over it. It was not really that easy at all. It took a lot of time and effort to master.

Now, I still have a lot of trouble lifting my right toe, but I have learned to look the other way. I sometimes feel that the more we stress something, the harder it is to get over it. It makes it difficult even to get through the smallest tasks of the day. But without stress, the whole ordeal has become simpler. I no longer regret getting up in the morning. I do not even dread it. Now it is routine to me, just as sleeping is routine. You know, it is true what they say. Stress does make everything worse. Then there is also heat that comes with humidity. I cannot believe I forgot about this one. I dread the humidity. It makes everything so sticky. With humidity, I cannot take hot showers at all. I take warm showers at most, and that too is a short affair. I am careful about not spending too much time in the shower. Instead of feeling clean, I end up feeling dirtier... all thanks to the humidity. Also, in humid weather, hot showers make me more exhausted. I am not really sure why that is.

I feel more weak and lethargic. Maybe it is the heat of the shower that gets to me. Whatever the case is, I sometimes get so exhausted that it is almost as if I am fainting. I have to crawl out of the bathroom on my hands and knees and head toward my bedroom. I am very glad to say that since I have started not to fret so much and take less stress. Things have become a lot better for me. Now, it does not feel that daunting. The summer heat, the haze, and the humidity have made summer my least favorite season. The other seasons are so much better. There is less heat and a sense of coolness. At least, we do not sweat all over the place. I still remember there was a time when I was a lot younger and completely oblivious of this illness that would shake up my entire life. I would play tennis for hours underneath the scorching sun. There was no concern about the humidity or the sweating that would follow. I knew I could easily hop into the shower as soon as I was done with the game. Now, I have to think twice. Actually, now I cannot play games, so there is no question of sweating underneath the sun.

As far as doing things is concerned, I must do it right away, and it exhausts me completely and quickly. For example, I cannot tell you how incredibly exhausting it is for me when I have to get dressed before visiting the doctor. I get all worked up and stressed out. Imagine having to live with it. I have figured out a way to deal with this. I start to get ready a long time before the appointment. This way, I can avoid the rush and hassle of getting ready at the very end.

I do not end up becoming ultra-stressed. I do not get fidgety. That is the new rule in my life - Plan and do not rush. Rushing does not take anywhere. I have come to accept it. It leads to stress, which is another enemy for us, so it is best that we keep calm and remain in control.

Chapter 9
Stress and Stressors

"The greatest weapon against stress is our ability to choose one thought over another."

-William James

Fatigue seems to follow me wherever I go. It seems I can never get rid of it, no matter how much I try or how much of a routine change I make. I feel it will always be there, no matter how much I try to shy away from it. It is just one of those things that I have to deal with, no matter what happens. So when I get tired, I am unable to be myself. I miss that part of me. I feel there is something always missing.

You know, I get stressed out by a lot of things. It is not only my illness that bothers me, but I also get bothered by what people think of me when they see me. There is a huge list of things that follow with it. I speak from personal experience when I say that stress is really a horrible deal. It takes away the best times and the best moments and leaves you with this feeling of agony and depression.

Something you cannot even move away from. It has all

of these physical effects on me. My legs tend to stiffen up, and I get spasticity, which I spoke about earlier. It tends to dominate me to the point where I cannot do anything effectively. I feel I am frozen to a spot and cannot walk. This makes me more frustrated and increases the level of stress. So it is kind of a vicious cycle. My muscles get so stiff that it becomes unbearable, and I cannot sit because of the pain. It takes all of my will and self-control to start screaming in pain. But I stifle it the best I can and move on.

I stretch my hamstrings, calf, and thigh muscles as much as I can. This helps me to move my legs. This makes my legs more mobile so that I do not have to face that stiffness again. It does help but not all the way through. There are moments when I have to sit for extended periods because standing up and walking around is not an option at all. To ease my leg muscles, I exercise by pressing the front of my toes into the floor.

There are also alternatives to this. For instance, sometimes I get up and stand for some time, even walk a couple of steps in any direction. It helps to keep the circulation going. My foot does not cramp up that much either. Like I said earlier, there are moments when I get severe anxiety attacks, and I get stressed out. I often try to take things in stride, but it is very hard I can tell you that. It is extremely hard. People keep saying that *live life to the fullest and have no stress*, but it is difficult to divert the mind from these thoughts. Throughout, my mind keeps entertaining these things until I feel I cannot block out my thoughts. I wish it were as easy as everyone says it is. I use Facebook, just like everyone else on this planet, but it is difficult for me. I read that my friends are happily married and enjoying their careers. They do not have to live with this life-changing illness and are free to live their life whichever way they choose, as the reigns of illness do not constrain them. It sometimes hurts me a lot.

So I wonder why me? What did I do? I do not recall hurting or wronging anyone. Even now, when these thoughts are running across my mind, I am not at all jealous. I do not envy my friends. I am happy for all the things they have. It is just that it leads me to feel depressed.

But I guess that is the way life works. I mean, what else is life then? We are never truly happy with what we have. I mean sure, there are a handful of us who are completely content, but as I said, they are a handful of people only. I suppose, on some level, it is completely natural to feel this way. If I am being plagued with bad times, then good times will also come. Make no mistake about it. I am certain of it. I know, for the moment, I have to endure this. It will not be long before the good time comes. The suffering will end, and I will have a completely normal life.

I have faith in the words of Jack London, "Life is not always a matter of holding good cards, but sometimes, playing a poor hand well."

Chapter 10
Depression

"Next time you're tempted to be upset, frustrated, offended, remind yourself, it is part of that ten percent of things in life you can't control, but you can control how you respond."

-Joel Osteen

You are now well-acquainted with the things I had to go through and still have to go through because of this illness. The symptoms, the test, the breakups, and the general trauma I have to endure. It is only natural that I wish this does not happen to me and that all illnesses are eradicated so that no one has to go through this suffering.

There were times when it got so bad that I felt drowning in the sea of depression. I even tried to take my life once. Doctors have prescribed anti-depression medications, but I have not taken any of them as yet. I do not want to, not because I think I will be labeled crazy or something along those lines. The thing is, I do not believe it will help to overcome depression. I believe it is only me who can pull myself out of depression. I can overcome this situation and do something more productive. This is something I feel in my heart. I repeatedly tell myself that tomorrow is a new day and will bring more greatness. I do not know what tomorrow will hold. We, as human beings, are fallible. We are not aware of what the next situation can bring. In fact, people's lives change within seconds. There is one defining moment, and the course of life is altered forever. So maybe mine will too. I am certainly hopeful that it will. They say time is a healer that heals all wounds. So, I believe time will also be my healer. There will come a time when things will get better, and all the sufferings will be worth it. I just have to wait patiently for that time.

Sickness is indeed a terrible thing. It breaks the best of people. It can send one down a very bad path. People who have major illnesses, such as cancer, may recover from it physically, but they report a slow deterioration in mental health. They feel that they are more prone to depressive disorder. There are times when they fall into such deep depression that they are unable to come out of it, and suicide seems to be the only option. Even people who have a heart attack, they report feeling depressed.

However, I believe this has a cure. Sickness is a terrible thing, but it can be lessened if one has a positive mindset. If we find the best in everything, we would not feel so depressed, and sickness would not be so prolonged either. Of course, this is a lot easier said than done. There are times when we are so caught up with all the bad stuff that life has thrown at us that we simply do not know if we can come out of it alive. Smiling through the pain is something that does not even cross our minds. At that point, if someone even tells us that we should be optimistic, we feel irritated. But we must force our self to have positive thoughts because the alternative is just too bad.

Sickness increases the worrisome thoughts of an individual. It can get to the point where we are constantly obsessed with it. The symptoms may not be so bad, but because of the constant worrying, it becomes difficult to think. For instance, if one has gloomy and negative thoughts of how things will happen, then not only will the future look gloomy and depressing, but the negative thoughts will also continue to overpower them. They will start to translate into our actions and words. This will lead to even more trouble.

I firmly believe that the brain is the best organ in our body. It is the best gift that has been given to us. It can control all our thoughts, emotions, and reactions, and has the power to make or break us. If you try to be calm and grateful for all the things you have, you will not have enough time to spend worrying over all the things that are not in your control. Then there is no question of depression or increased sickness. There is only peace and calm.

Trust me; it is not that easy to find things around you that make you feel grateful, especially when you are stuck in the kind of situation that I find myself in. There are times when I am too busy focusing on the next step to take out the time to list the things that I am grateful for. There are also times when I feel there is only negativity around me and no positive things.

But of course, that is not the case. Think back to the last time you were in a bad situation. Did you have friends and family around you to support you? Did you have food on the table? Did you have enough money to be able to pay your bills? Did you have a roof over your head? Yes, you did. You see, you do have things to be grateful for in life. The thing is, it is never completely black and white. It just takes some time and patience to be able to come through to the side where we are in a position to list down the things that we are grateful for. Perhaps that is the key to making us get to the other side - the side where we are grateful and not so bothered about the sickness. I sincerely hope we can all make it there.

Chapter 11
Meeting People

"Each person you meet influences your mental universe in a way that has the potential to make a substantial impact upon the causality of the intellectual development of an entire species."

-Abhijit Naskar

I have this thing. I get nervous around people. It is not what you are thinking. I do not shy away from people. It is just that I get stressed out when I have to meet someone new. I do not know why. Perhaps it is the fact that I am not sure how it will play out or whether we will connect. But I think a major part of it has to do with the fact that I wonder what they will think of me.

I know this is something I should not care about. I mean, what is the probability that the people I meet will stick around in my life? Most of my ex-girlfriends did not. Besides, even if they did, it was not their concern to decide what I do with my life or how I handle my illness. That power solely rests with me. Despite knowing all this and rationalizing, it still freaks me out. I really wish it does not.

I envy people who are living their lives, completely untainted by other people's points of view. I badly want to be like them. I also pacify myself. I tell myself that this should not bother me at all and that I should rise above such things. I am not a child who should succumb to peer pressure. I am an independent person who is fighting my own battles. Time and time again, I counsel myself on this. But I am only human. I fail to live up to those expectations - my own expectations.

The second I hear that someone new is coming to meet me or I am going to meet them, my reaction is instantaneous. It is almost as if it is a reflex. All of these thoughts start to race through my head. I wonder if they will like me. Would I match up to their expectations? Would they feel sorry for me? It is as if I cannot stop thinking. I am just unable to pause my thoughts, take a deep breath, and let it all go. What will they think of me? It is this cycle of anxiety and nervousness that is critical in my head. I can do absolutely nothing to block it. It frustrates me like nothing else.

You know this quote by Jonathan Davis, *"I don't care what people think or say about me, I know who I am."* I want to live by it. I want the reflection of this quote in my every action. I just hope I can get there sooner, for the peace of mind that this offer will be unparalleled by anything else. It will set me free.

Chapter 12
Education

"The key to realizing a dream is to focus not on success but significance, and then even the small steps and little victories along your path will take on greater meaning."

-Oprah Winfrey

After I graduated from college, I started going to medical school. I think I have mentioned this earlier as well. I felt as if my future was finally opening up, and nothing could bring me down. I was on cloud nine. Things were going according to plan. I guess that is the thing that hints that plans are being followed effectively. They sort of lull people into this false sense of confidence that nothing can go wrong. That was what happened to me.

I was unfortunate in the sense that I was able to last only one year in medical school. It was then that all hell broke loose. My life completely turned, and I was none the wiser. My walking became extremely difficult, and I was unsure of what was happening to me. I tried to shrug it off. I told myself that it would go away with time. But then other things started to happen. My vision was acting up, and this was pretty unusual. I was having double-vision episodes in some instances. As a result, my balance, concentration, and cognition were completely off. I loved to play tennis. I have discussed this earlier as well. But now, the very sport I loved to play earlier was completely off-limits to me. It was a dream that would never be realized. I did try it. It was not something easy for me to give up something that was so dear to me. I could not. But even when I tried to play, it was a lost cause. There were times when I could see not one but two tennis balls hurtling toward me. As a result, I ended up swinging in midair at the wrong ball.

Time went on, and my health continued to deteriorate. It got worse; I will not lie. There were sleepless nights and tiring days. There were times when I wondered if I would ever live to see the next day. But here I am. I think the highlight of my life was when a group of students saw me try to take my life. Imagine, if this is the highlight, then what would be the down-low? There are moments of my life that I wish never to recall. I suppose dealing with the illness in the initial stages is one of them. So, I continued to withdraw from society. I wanted nothing to do with it. I did not belong, and I could see that in the stares of the people as they watched me limping. There was a time I felt as if I could not take this anymore. I was so lost until I spoke to my cousin. He was a medical doctor and pursuing his Ph.D. He came to see me and ask me how I was coping with the setback of leaving medical school. I told him everything and asked for his advice. I wanted to do something academically. He, along with his girlfriend, gave me good advice. They encouraged me to pursue a master's degree. Since they both were pursuing a Ph.D. degree, it made sense that they would tell me to do the same. But their idea resonated with me. I could see myself as a master's student, and so I latched on to this idea.

I got admission in a graduate school and began my Masters in Biology. I lived on campus for an entire year, as my apartment was located at a prime location. I enjoyed going to classes and learning about Biology. For my thesis topic, by some stroke of luck, I met with a professor whose husband also suffered from MS. I felt it was natural to disclose to her that I too had MS I wanted to do my thesis on this topic so that it could be my contribution to my disease. So we came to a resolution. My thesis focused on the potential or possibility of using statin drugs to fight the inflammation associated with MS as a potential MS therapy. It was fun. The research led me to a renewed understanding of myself and this disease. I ended my thesis and got a job as a science editor at an academic test prep company. My job was to write and edit sections of selected textbooks. These would then be published. The commute was fairly easy. I went from home to the office through a company tailored to help people with disabilities, such as myself.

I am a big advocate for this service. I believe it is a godsend. I cannot even tell you the stress that had been cut from my life as a result of this service. At first, it was all about public transportation. I had to take the subway, walk up and down the stairs, or take a taxi. With my legs, it was not always possible.

By then, stress was mitigated from my life. Well, not completely, but to a large degree. I was at a lot more ease and could commute effectively. I even had the opportunity of sleeping in the car. It was that safe. I used this service whenever I had to go to the city for either class or any type of appointment. Also, gone were the days when I had to be dependent on other people, such as my family or friends to take me to other places. I was now independent, as much as I could be. All thanks to this service!

Chapter 13
Spasticity

"The problem contains the solution."

-Michael Bierut

I have talked about this repeatedly and will say it again. It still feels as if I cannot come to terms with it. For several years after I was diagnosed with MS, I had balance and coordination issues. I could not stand upright. I had trouble walking on my own. Eventually, I could only walk with the help of a cane. The thing is, I was always led to believe that this is the fate of an MS patient that they are crippled forever.

This is not what a physical therapist told me, though. He said that I suffer from a gait abnormality known as foot drop, which is a form of paralysis. This means my leg with foot drop is like an added weight. It is tough to carry the leg when one is walking. This was more the case when I wanted to walk upstairs. This was where the real work began. I had to raise my thigh so that I could step forward. This made it so difficult. I cannot convey to you the problems I faced from something so simple as walking. This is one of the reasons why banisters and handrails are so badly needed for people like me. I could not imagine climbing up the stairs without this support. It helped me to maintain my balance. God forbid, had these facilities not been there; it might even become fatal for me to climb. If I ever came across staircases that did not have banisters, I simply turned away. There was no way I could climb up these steps at all. Now I have come to understand that I also suffer from spasticity. This diagnosis is kind of a relief for me because it is not related to MS at all, and it can get better. I have become proactive about this and take every necessary measure to better my condition.

The day my physical therapist told me that I do not have foot drop but increased spasticity, I went home, and the first thing I did was order grab bars. This time, I did not get depressed over my illness. Instead, I channeled that energy into bolting those bars in my walls. This made walking so much easier for me. I know this for a fact. Now that the bars have been installed, I see improvement in my daily productivity. I don't have to worry much longer.

Chapter 14
Determination

"The human capacity for burden is like bamboo- far more flexible than you'd ever believe at first glance."

-Jodi Picoult

It has been 17 years since I was first diagnosed. This journey has been nothing short of a roller coaster ride. I have no job or happiness in my life. I believe I am living in depression. There is no way out. I can see no light ahead of me. There is only darkness.

Every time I feel there is a direction, I turn toward it. I hope there is a door that will eventually lead me somewhere. But for the past 17 years, I have been disappointed. The door opens only to reveal a wall that is impossible to break down. Every time I get saddened and angry with myself and my life. I see around me. My class fellows from my first year of medical school have accomplished a lot. I wonder what kind of a doctor I would be, had I not been hit with this crippling disease. Perhaps, I would one day save the lives of people, just as the doctors are trying to save mine.

The days continue to pass. But no matter whatever I attempt, the door remains shut. Am I worried? Sometimes I am. But most of the time, I do not let it affect me in any way. I do not want to give so much power to this intruder. The one that has managed to take over my life. I believe I am in my control; not my MS. This disease has given me hell. It has taken away so much from me - my entire life, my hopes, my dreams, and my aspirations. But I am a fighter. Gone are the days when I would get so depressed that I would consider ending my life. I still have my mind and can use it to my advantage. Thinking positive is the way to go. I have always been a fighter, and there is no better time than now to stand firm and put up a fight. I do not give up now. I have a can-do attitude in life, and I do whatever I can to stand strong against MS.

I will fight; that is my promise. I will make a way out for myself. Resilience, perseverance, and commitment make me who I am. No one, I repeat, no one can take that away from me.

SAURABH CHOWDHRY

www.ingramcontent.com/pod-product-compliance
Lightning Source LLC
Chambersburg PA
CBHW021158090426
42740CB00008B/1143